GREAT ESCAPES

THE UNDERGROUND RAILROAD

Dennis Brindell Fradin

Published by Marshall Cavendish Benchmark
An imprint of Marshall Cavendish Corporation

Website: www.marshallcavendish.us

This publication represents the opinions and views of the author based on Dennis
Brindell Fradin's personal experience, knowledge, and research. The information in
this book serves as a general guide only. The author and publisher have used their best
efforts in preparing this book and disclaim liability rising directly and indirectly from the
use and application of this book.

Other Marshall Cavendish Offices:

Marshall Cavendish International (Asia) Private Limited, 1 New Industrial Road,
Singapore 536196 • Marshall Cavendish International (Thailand) Co Ltd. 253 Asoke,
12th Flr, Sukhumvit 21 Road, Klongtoey Nua, Wattana, Bangkok 10110, Thailand
• Marshall Cavendish (Malaysia) Sdn Bhd, Times Subang, Lot 46, Subang Hi-Tech
Industrial Park, Batu Tiga, 40000 Shah Alam, Selangor Darul Ehsan, Malaysia

Marshall Cavendish is a trademark of Times Publishing Limited

All websites were available and accurate when this book was sent to press.

Library of Congress Cataloging-in-Publication Data

Fradin, Dennis B.
The Underground Railroad / Dennis Brindell Fradin.
p. cm. — (Great escapes)
Includes bibliographical references and index.
ISBN 978-1-60870-476-7 (print)—ISBN 978-1-60870-697-6 (ebook)
1. Underground Railroad—Juvenile literature. 2. Fugitive slaves—United
States—History—19th century—Juvenile literature. 3. Antislavery
movements—United States—History—19th century—Juvenile literature. 4.
Abolitionists—United States—History—19th century—Juvenile literature.
I. Title.
E450.F775 2012
973.7'115—dc22
2010040063

Senior Editor: Deborah Grahame-Smith
Publisher: Michelle Bisson
Art Director: Anahid Hamparian
Series Designer: Kay Petronio

Photo research by Linda Sykes

The photographs in this book are used by permission and through the courtesy of:
© adam james/Alamy: cover; The Granger Collection: 4, 8, 11, 14, 20, 23, 24, 26, 32,
38, 42, 47, 49, 54, 60-61; Louie Psihoyos/Science Faction/Corbis: 16; Richard Cummins/
Corbis: 18; Schomburg Center/Art Resource, NY: 22; Rebecca James: 29 (top); ©Michael
Snell/Alamy: 29 (bottom); Superstock: 33; *Narrative of William W. Brown, an American
Slave*/University of North Carolina, Chapel Hill: 34; Corbis/Bettmann: 40; National
Geographic Collection/Getty Images: 44; Jerry Pinckney/National Geographic Collection/
Getty Images: 62.

Printed in Malaysia (T)
135642

CONTENTS

Slave owners made no attempt to keep families intact at auctions. Each slave was sold to the highest bidder.

INTRODUCTION

"IS THEE A SLAVE?"

Born in Kentucky in 1815, a slave named William grew up on a Missouri tobacco farm with his sister, three brothers, and their mother. By the time William was nineteen his family had been broken apart because their owners needed money. His sister was sold to a man in Mississippi. His three brothers were sold. His mother was sent down to Louisiana and sold. Her parting advice to William was that he should escape. "Try to get your liberty!" she told him.

William was sold soon after to steamboat captain Enoch Price of Saint Louis, Missouri. William's job was to serve the Price family in their home and also to wait on the steamboat passengers. William always acted polite and happy in front of the Prices, but not an hour passed that he didn't think of his mother's advice.

His chance to escape came on January 1, 1834, when Captain Price's steamboat was docked at Cincinnati, Ohio. While the cargo was being unloaded, William slipped off the vessel carrying a trunk, as if his owner had ordered him to take it ashore. He entered a woodland area, where he hid until sunset. At nightfall he began walking northward, keeping to his course by following the North Star. It was New Year's Day of 1834, and William hoped that in a few weeks he would be starting a new life in Canada.

Ohio didn't allow slavery, so by that state's laws William was already free once he stepped on its soil. But an old United States law—the Fugitive Slave Act of 1793—permitted owners and slave hunters to "seize or arrest" runaways in any state and return them to slavery. In case Captain Price sent slave hunters after him into Ohio, William traveled by night. On the night of January 1 he walked 25 miles (40 kilometers). He planned to walk north up to Cleveland, Ohio. From there he would sail across Lake Erie to Canada, where slave catchers were not permitted to go.

William walked about 10 miles (16 km) a night, then spent the daylight hours resting in barns and caves where he wouldn't be spotted. But it was the dead of winter, and the weather was very cold. Except for some turnips and corn he found, food was scarce. Then, on about the fifth day of his journey, he ran into a sleet storm that froze his clothes to his body. He developed a terrible cough and ran a fever, and his legs grew so numb that he could hardly feel them as he trudged through the ice and snow. Three days passed and he had nothing at all to eat.

If he didn't find help soon, William realized, he would die. He came out of hiding in broad daylight and made his way to a road. Watching from behind some fallen trees, he studied the people passing by in the hope of finding someone who might come to his aid. Soon an elderly man wearing a long coat and a broad-brimmed hat approached, leading a horse. William came out from behind the fallen trees and stumbled toward him.

"Is thee a slave?" the man asked him.

William admitted that he was a runaway slave badly in need of help. The old man said that many people in this part of

Ohio favored slavery and might try to capture William for the reward money that his master would undoubtedly pay. He told William to remain out of sight while he went home to fetch his covered wagon. Then he would take William to his farm, where he could recover. William agreed, and the old man hurried off to get his covered wagon.

While he waited, William hoped the elderly man was part of the Underground Railroad. This name was just coming into style to describe people who provided food, shelter, and other kinds of help for runaway slaves. The old man certainly had *acted* as if he were part of the Underground Railroad, but he could have been pretending. It was true: Many people would want to capture William for the reward money. Perhaps at that very moment the old man was rounding up some friends to help catch William.

A half-hour went by, and the old gentleman did not return. A full hour passed, and still there was no sign of him. William thought about leaving his hiding place by the side of the road and continuing on alone, but he lacked the strength to go anywhere. He could only trust that the old man really wanted to help him.

After William had been waiting an hour and a half, he saw a covered wagon coming down the road. The old man was driving it. In a moment, William would find out whether the man intended to capture or help him.

Slave quarters aboard a ship. Crossing the ocean was perilous in such cramped conditions, and many Africans did not survive the ordeal.

SLAVERY: "THE NEXT THING TO HELL"

"Now [that] I've been free, I know what a dreadful condition slavery is," explained famous Underground Railroad conductor Harriet Tubman, several years after escaping from bondage. "I think slavery is the next thing to hell. If a person would send another into bondage, he would, it appears to me, be bad enough to send him into hell, if he could."

The First Slaves in the Americas: The Indians

When Harriet Tubman said this in 1856, the Americas had already experienced more than three hundred years of slavery. Indians were the first slaves in the Americas. Explorer Christopher Columbus began the evil practice while on his famous voyage of 1492 to 1493. Columbus liked the Native Americans, calling them a gentle people who "offer to share with anyone." Because the Indians were so peaceful, Columbus added, "they would make fine servants. With fifty men we could make them do whatever we want." Columbus and his men kidnapped several Indians as slaves and forced them to return with them to Spain.

Following Columbus's famous voyage, Europeans settled in the New World. They came in quest of gold and silver and to establish ranches and farms. As Columbus had advised, they captured Indians and forced them to mine treasure for them and do their farm work. Millions of Indian slaves died of mistreatment and overwork, and in battles with Europeans. Whole Indian tribes were wiped out.

Slaves from Africa

As the numbers of American Indians dwindled, European colonists in the Americas turned to Africa for slaves. From the 1500s to the 1800s as many as 15 million Africans were captured and forcibly shipped to the New World. About 2 million of them died during the ocean crossing. Those who survived the voyage in the cramped, disease-ridden ships were sold into slavery in North, South, and Central America and in the islands called the West Indies.

In what became the United States, African-American slavery began in 1619. That year twenty African people landed in Jamestown, Virginia, which had been established in 1607 as England's first permanent town in the present-day United States. As the colonial population grew, more and more African slaves were imported to do the colonists' work. By 1776—the year England's thirteen colonies became the United States of America—500,000 out of the new country's 2.5 million people were black slaves. One out of every five people in the new nation was a slave.

The North Ends Slavery, but the South Doesn't

Slaves were not distributed evenly throughout the United States. The northern part of the country developed as a region of small farms and towns. Slave labor was not as important to the region's economy and way of life, so the North had relatively few slaves. The South, on the other hand, developed as a region of big farms and plantations where tobacco, rice, sugar, cotton, and indigo were grown. Southern landowners believed that using slave labor was the most profitable way to cultivate their

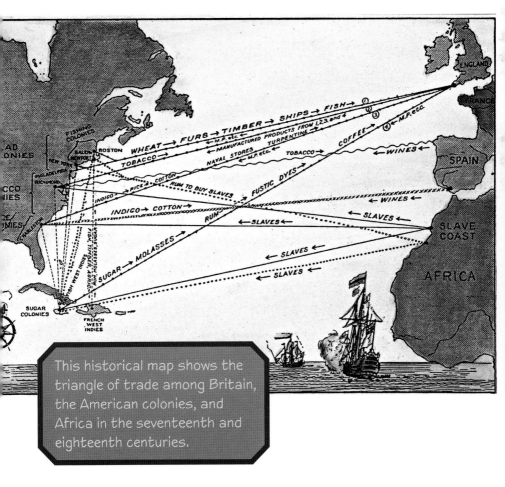

This historical map shows the triangle of trade among Britain, the American colonies, and Africa in the seventeenth and eighteenth centuries.

lands and grow their crops, and so the South had the bulk of the nation's slaves.

Soon after the birth of the United States, the Northern states began to outlaw slavery. Massachusetts was first, in 1780. The rest of the original Northern states followed. When Ohio, Indiana, Illinois, and other new Northern states joined the nation, they, too, banned slavery. By the mid-1800s slavery had been ended in the Northern United States.

Meanwhile, in the Southern states, slavery was growing. Some white Southern planters owned hundreds of African slaves. When new Southern states such as Louisiana, Mississippi, and Texas were added to the Union, they, too, allowed slavery. By 1830 the population of the United States reached 13 million, of which 2 million—nearly one sixth of the total—were black slaves in the South.

Black Northerners were treated unfairly by the white majority. They were generally not allowed to vote. They "were either excluded from railway cars, stagecoaches, and steamboats, or assigned to special [segregated] sections," explains historian Eugene Berwanger. "They sat, when permitted, in secluded and remote corners of theaters and lecture halls. They could not enter most hotels, restaurants, and resorts, except as servants. They prayed in 'Negro pews' in the white churches. Moreover, they were educated in segregated schools, punished in segregated prisons, nursed in segregated hospitals, and buried in segregated cemeteries." Despite the bias many of them had against African Americans, Northerners drew the line at slavery.

Also by 1830, more than 300,000 African Americans were free. Most of the "free blacks," as they were called, lived in the North, but there were small numbers of them in the South, too. Blacks were free for a variety of reasons. Some were set free by the terms of their owners' wills. Some managed to save enough money to buy their freedom out of slavery. And some escaped to states that didn't allow slavery.

Slave Life

Drudgery, pain, and heartbreak were lifelong companions of most slaves. Owners could force them to work inhuman hours, whip them for breaking the rules, and even kill them if they struck a white person. Slaves usually had nothing to call their own—not even themselves. Slaves who were caught running away were sometimes charged with the crime of "stealing themselves and their clothes."

There was an aspect of being a piece of property that slaves especially dreaded. A healthy slave in 1850 could sell for $1,000—equal to about $25,000 in today's money. Owners who needed cash often sold their slaves, as happened to William's family, described in the Introduction. Families were broken up at slave sales. More than sixty years after the event, Josiah Henson still felt the heartbreak of being parted from his family at a slave auction when he was five years old:

> The crowd collected round the [auction] stand, the huddling group of Negroes, the agony of my mother. I can shut my eyes and see them all.
>
> My brothers and sisters were bid off first, one by one, while my mother, paralyzed by grief, held me by the hand. Her turn came, and she was bought by Isaac Riley of Montgomery County. Then I was offered to the purchasers. My mother, distracted with the thought of parting forever from all her children, while

Field slaves working in the "rice colonies" of the South. Rice, cotton, and indigo dye were in great demand in Europe and shipped out of the ports of Charleston, South Carolina.

the bidding for me was going on, fell at [Riley's] feet, and clung to his knees, entreating him to buy her *baby* as well as herself, and spare to her one of her little ones. This man [answered] her with such violent blows and kicks, as to reduce her to creeping out of his reach, and mingling the groan of bodily suffering with the sob of a broken heart. I seem to see and hear my poor weeping mother now.

Slaves were denied many of the rights we now consider basic. Owners were afraid that educated slaves would exchange messages and plan a rebellion. That is why the Southern states passed laws that made educating slaves illegal. For example, according to an 1830 Louisiana law, the punishment for teaching slaves to read and write was imprisonment for up to one year.

Slaves could go only where their owners permitted. To leave home they needed a pass. Any white person who encountered an unaccompanied black person could demand to see his or her pass. Slaves without a pass were hauled back to their owners or thrown in jail.

Slaves sometimes were told by their owners when and whom to marry. From birth slave children belonged to their mother's owner. To own any valuable babies who might be born, slaveholders wanted their female slaves to marry early and have lots of children.

If they were permitted to worship at all, slaves had to attend a church of their owner's choosing. White ministers scared the slaves into obedience by saying that God had made white people the masters and black people the workers.

Three Kinds of Slaves

There were three kinds of slaves. Some masters let a few of their slaves "hire their own time." These were slaves with special skills—carpenters, barbers, blacksmiths, hairdressers, and dressmakers—who were allowed to make their own work arrangements. Carpenters went from plantation to plantation working on construction jobs, while dressmakers traveled about seeking sewing work. Such slaves had to give most of their earnings to their owners, but they could keep a little for themselves. Slaves who hired their own time often accumulated enough money to buy their own clothing, food, and perhaps even a house.

Since they were allowed to travel around, what prevented slaves who hired their own time from escaping? For one thing most of them had families they would be reluctant to leave

Slaves who hired their own time earned small sums of money for themselves. So did house slaves and field slaves who worked on Sundays, the slaves' one day off. By saving nickels and dimes over many years, some slaves eventually were able to buy their way out of slavery.

A copper tag issued in 1831 identifies "Servant No. 1890." Slaves not wearing tags or carrying identification papers were jailed.

behind. For another there was the fear of punishment if they were caught.

"House slaves" were the second type of slave. Female house slaves cooked the food for their owners and their families. They cleaned the house, washed clothes, sewed, and performed much of the child care. Male house slaves chopped wood, worked as handymen, and drove their owners around in carriages.

House slaves in some ways had a better life than most other slaves. They got to eat the leftover scraps off their owners' plates. They wore their owners' old hand-me-down clothing. They slept in the "big house," as their owners' home was called. In other ways their lives were harder. They were watched very closely, and they had to be available to their owners at any hour of the day or night.

By far the largest number of slaves worked in the fields. These "field slaves" planted, grew, and harvested their owners' crops. Field slaves, including children as young as eight, worked from sunup to sundown. They lived in log huts. Once a year they were provided with flimsy clothing that was soon in tatters. Their usual food was cornmeal and bacon, although some were allowed to supplement their meager diet by fishing, hunting, and growing a vegetable garden.

Masters who owned one or two slaves might work in the fields alongside them. Owners of many slaves employed a field boss called an overseer to supervise them. Overseers were armed with whips and guns. A slave who attempted to run away or who tried to fight the overseer or another white person might get shot. Slaves were whipped for a variety of reasons, from not being out in the fields by sunrise to not picking enough cotton by day's end. All his life Frederick Douglass was haunted by the memory of his aunt Hester being whipped by their owner for going out at night to meet a young man on a nearby plantation. Douglass wrote in his autobiography:

The interior of a typical slave cabin. Owners considered their castoff furniture, clothing, and bedding adequate for a slave family's use.

I have often been awakened at the dawn of day by the most heart-rending shrieks of an aunt of mine, whom he used to tie up, and whip upon her back till she was covered with blood. No tears, no prayers from his victim seemed to move his heart from its bloody purpose. The louder she screamed, the harder he whipped; and where the blood ran fastest, there he whipped longest. Not until overcome by fatigue would he cease to swing the blood-clotted cowskin. I remember the first time I ever witnessed this horrible exhibition. I was quite a child, but I shall never forget it whilst I remember anything. It was the blood-stained gate, the entrance to the hell of slavery, through which I was about to pass.

Frederick Douglass would not remain behind the bloody gate of slavery all his life. And neither would thousands of other slaves who escaped on what became known as the Underground Railroad.

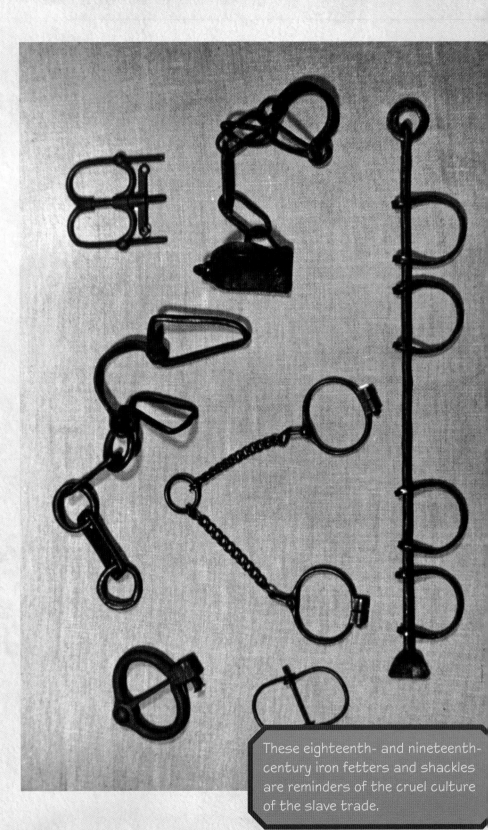

These eighteenth- and nineteenth-century iron fetters and shackles are reminders of the cruel culture of the slave trade.

"THERE MUST BE AN UNDERGROUND RAILROAD"

Like other oppressed people, from time to time groups of slaves rebelled. Since they could not read or write, they organized rebellions by word of mouth. Slaves sent on errands would pass the news that on a certain day the black people in a neighborhood would attack their masters.

The earliest known slave revolt in what became the United States was planned in Gloucester County, Virginia, in 1663. The rebels included white servants as well as black slaves. Authorities learned about the revolt before it could be carried out, however. Several people involved in the plot were executed.

Back when all thirteen colonies allowed slavery, revolts occurred in the Northern part of the country, too. For example, during New York City's Slave Rebellion of 1712, slaves burned houses and killed nine white people. Soldiers were sent in to squash the rebellion, and twenty-one slaves were executed.

Three major slave uprisings took place in the early 1800s. Gabriel Prosser, a slave on a Virginia tobacco plantation, led the first. With help from his two brothers, Prosser recruited one thousand followers. In the summer of 1800 the rebels gathered near Richmond, the capital of Virginia. They planned to kill local slaveholders and seize Richmond. However, the plot was uncovered, and soldiers were called in. Gabriel, his brothers, and about thirty-five other slaves were hanged, ending Gabriel's Rebellion.

The subject of this nineteenth-century painting, titled *The Escaped Slave*, is thought to be Gabriel Prosser.

Twenty-two years later, Denmark Vesey led a revolt in South Carolina. Vesey had grown up a slave, but in 1800 he won $1,500 in a lottery. He spent $600 of it to buy his freedom. Now a "free black," Vesey still hated slavery. He became a minister and convinced many of his church members to assist with his plan. On a Sunday in 1822 his followers, including nine thousand slaves and free blacks, planned to set fire to white people's homes in Charleston. As with Gabriel Prosser, the plan was discovered. Denmark Vesey was hanged, along with dozens of his followers.

CLASS No. 1.

Comprises those prisoners who were found guilty and executed.

Prisoners Names.	Owners' Names.	Time of Commit.	How Disposed of.
Peter	James Poyas	June 18	
Ned	Gov. T. Bennett,	do.	Hanged on Tuesday
Rolla	do.	do	the 2d July, 1822,
Batteau	do.	do.	on Blake's lands,
Denmark Vesey	A free black man	22	near Charleston.
Jessy	Thos. Blackwood	23	
John	Elias Horry	July 5	Do. on the Lines near
Gullah Jack	Paul Pritchard	do.	Ch.; Friday July 12.
Mingo	Wm. Harth	June 21	
Lot	Forrester		
Joe	P. L. Jore		
Julius	Thos. Forrest		
Tom	Mrs. Russell		
Smart	Robt. Anderson		
John	John Robertson		
Robert	do.		
Adam	do.		
Polydore	Mrs. Faber	do	
Bacchus	Benj. Hammet	do.	near Charleston,
Dick	Wm. Sims	13	on Friday, 26th
Pharaoh	— Thompson	do.	July.
Jemmy	Mrs. Clement	18	
Mauidore	Mordecai Cohen	19	
Dean	— Mitchell	do.	
Jack	Mrs. Purcell	12	
Bellisle	Est. of Jos. Yates	18	
Naphur	do.	do.	
Adam	do.	do.	
Jacob	John S. Glen	16	
Charles	John Billings	18	

This printed record lists thirty-five men who were hanged for planning a revolt in 1822 in Charleston, South Carolina. Denmark Vesey is number five on the list.

Nat Turner led the bloodiest of the two hundred slave revolts in the United States before the Civil War. A slave in Virginia's Southampton County, Turner was a religious man who believed that his purpose in life was to liberate his people. In August of 1831 Turner and a few followers went from house to house in Southampton County, freeing slaves and killing their white masters.

Nat Turner's army of slaves and free blacks soon grew to sixty armed men. Fifty-five white people were killed in the Nat Turner Rebellion of 1831. Soldiers were sent to capture Turner, who hid in a swamp for six weeks. He was finally caught and hanged, along with more than fifty of his followers. Out of revenge for Nat Turner's actions, white gangs killed hundreds of African Americans, many of whom had no connection with the revolt.

The Nat Turner Rebellion shocked the nation and served as a catalyst for the abolition movement in the United States.

Slave Escapes

Although they killed dozens of white people and terrified thousands more, the revolts did little to end slavery. With seven white people for every one of them, the slaves were too greatly outnumbered to triumph in battle. The white people also had a trained army and the latest weapons to help put down slave revolts.

There was another way that slaves could break their chains. They could escape to the Northern states or to Canada, neither of which allowed slavery. This was easier said than done.

For one thing, in the South, "slave patrols" rode around at night looking for escaped slaves. The white men of an area took turns serving as patrols. Fugitive slaves also had to contend with dog packs. Trained to track down human beings, the dogs were let loose as soon as a master realized that a slave was missing.

Fugitives who evaded the slave patrols and dog packs were still not out of danger. Owners advertised in newspapers and sent telegraph messages offering rewards for the capture of their runaway slaves. A typical reward was $100—equal to

As mentioned in connection with William the runaway, the Fugitive Slave Act of 1793 allowed owners and slave hunters to "seize or arrest" escaped slaves in any state, North or South. But because of the difficulty and expense of catching and returning them, fugitives generally were not pursued once they reached the Northern states. They were either caught while they were still in the South or not at all. This would change in 1850, though.

$2,500 in today's money. Sometimes as much as $500 was offered for a slave's return. Gun-carrying slave hunters made a living by tracking down fugitive slaves and returning them to their masters.

Captured runaways were dealt with harshly. Their masters whipped them brutally and in some cases branded them like cattle. Often slaves who had run away were sold to new owners far from friends and family.

Depending on their starting point, slaves often had to travel hundreds of miles to reach free soil. They had to cross rivers, climb hills, pass through snake- and alligator-infested swamps, and find their way through forests. In the wintertime they had to make their way across vast fields of snow. They knew nothing about maps, yet they knew they must maintain a northerly course.

A slave escape often began on a Saturday night. That was because most slaves had Sunday off. Not until Monday would their owners notice that they were missing, so searches and placement of newspaper ads were delayed.

Runaway slaves discovered a way to make sure they were heading north. Because it is located directly over the Earth's North Pole, Polaris, also called the North Star, always remains due north in the sky. If they could see the North Star ahead of them, the fugitives knew they were going northward. Josiah Henson expressed how fugitive slaves felt about this star when he wrote: "The North Star—blessed be God for setting it in the heavens. I thought of it as my guide to the land of promise." What about nights when clouds hid the North Star? Then the runaways had another way to make sure they were heading in the right direction. They looked for the moss that grew thickest on the northern side of trees.

ONA JUDGE, RUNAWAY FROM THE WASHINGTONS

Thousands of slaves escaped in the country's early years. In 1796 Ona Judge, a slave belonging to George Washington's family, escaped from the President's House in Philadelphia, which was the U.S. capital at that time. President Washington located Ona in New Hampshire, but she refused to return to the Washingtons. Since New Hampshire had ended slavery in 1783, Ona lived the rest of her life as a free woman.

A fugitive slave might walk about 10 miles (16 km) over the course of a night. Once the sun rose runaways were in great danger of being seen and captured, so they rested in hidden places such as caves, abandoned buildings and barns, trees, or overgrown fields during the daytime. For food they raided beehives, picked berries, and took vegetables and fruits from gardens.

Birth of the Underground Railroad

Because few records were kept, we don't know much about slave escapes of the 1600s and 1700s. We know much more about the Underground Railroad, which arose in the early 1800s. The Underground Railroad was not underground, nor was it a railroad. It was an informal network of homes and other hiding places where slaves stopped for food, fresh clothing, and rest on their northward journey. The term *Underground Railroad* was also applied to the thousands of people who sheltered and otherwise aided escaped slaves.

How did the Underground Railroad get its start? That remains a mystery, as do the questions of when and where it began. Probably for as long as slavery has existed there have been people with a sense of justice who have helped slaves escape. However, the name *Underground Railroad* seems to have come into use around the 1830s, when real railroads were being established in the United States.

According to one story the name originated in Newport (present-day Fountain City), Indiana. The home of Levi and Katie Coffin in Newport was an important stopping place for runaways, with secret rooms where fugitives could hide from slave catchers. It was said that sometime around 1830, slave hunters from Kentucky tracked a group of runaways to the vicinity of the Coffins' home. When the slaves disappeared into hidden passages, a frustrated slave catcher allegedly remarked: "There must be an underground railroad, and

The home of Levi and Katie Coffin, who sheltered more than three thousand fugitive slaves.

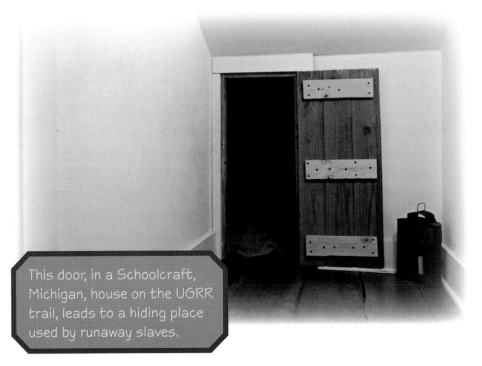

This door, in a Schoolcraft, Michigan, house on the UGRR trail, leads to a hiding place used by runaway slaves.

Levi Coffin must be its president, and his home the Grand Central Station."

The name *Underground Railroad* stuck because it perfectly described how fugitive slaves seemed to vanish off the face of the Earth in certain places. A number of railroad expressions were coined to describe people who aided slaves on the UGRR (as the Underground Railroad was known for short). Southerners who arranged for slaves to escape were called *ticket agents*. People like Harriet Tubman who led slaves northward were called *conductors*. Levi and Katie Coffin and others who sheltered fugitive slaves were called *stationmasters*, while their homes were *depots* or *stations*.

The fleeing slaves were referred to as *passengers*, *shipments*, *cargo*, *freight*, and *goods*. If passengers were captured along the way, it was said that *the train was run off the track*. Usually, though, the *brakemen*, as people who helped fugitives once they reached free soil were called, reported a *smooth trip*. Many people simply referred to anyone involved with helping slaves escape as an Underground Railroad *agent*.

These railroad expressions protected people who took part in helping fugitive slaves. Imagine, for example, that a conductor was overheard talking about "cargo being taken to Canada." He or she could claim to be discussing a new railway line—not a slave escape.

Since a fugitive slave could walk about 10 miles (16 km) in a night, stations ideally would be located at roughly 10-mile (16-km) intervals. The way it worked in actuality, however, was that in some areas UGRR stations were clustered together, while in other areas they were dozens of miles apart. The Quakers, members of a religious faith that strongly opposed slavery, sometimes volunteered to open depots in places where they were lacking. Many people wrongly believe that most Underground Railroad workers were white. Although both black and white people helped escaped slaves, most Underground

THE QUAKERS AND SLAVERY

A religion called the Society of Friends was founded in England by George Fox in the mid-1600s. Called Friends or more commonly Quakers, members became known for their hatred of war and their belief that all people have a bit of God in them and deserve respect. In 1784 the Quakers became the first religious denomination in the United States to end slaveholding among its members. The Quakers also were a leading faith in establishing Underground Railroad depots and conducting slaves to freedom.

Railroad workers were actually African Americans, both free and enslaved.

Between 1830 and 1850 the slave population grew enormously in the South. It rose from 2 million to 3.2 million in those twenty years. As slavery grew so did the Underground Railroad in response. There were hundreds of Underground Railroad agents in 1830. By 1850 the number had grown to several thousand.

How could escaped slaves tell which houses were Underground Railroad stations? Before leaving one station, runaways were told by the stationmasters where they would find the next resting place. UGRR stationmasters also used signals. In some places a lantern attached to a hitching post was a signal that fugitive slaves were welcome. To gain admittance to certain UGRR stations, passengers were instructed to use a secret knock.

By the 1830s and 1840s more than two thousand slaves were escaping from the South every year. Although many of them escaped with the UGRR's help, many others escaped

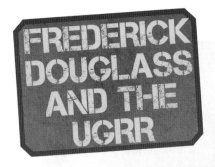

FREDERICK DOUGLASS AND THE UGRR

Frederick Douglass was born on Maryland's Eastern Shore in about 1817. When Frederick was nine years old his owner's wife, whom he later described as "a kind and tender-hearted woman," broke the law by teaching him to read and write. In 1838 Douglass escaped to freedom in New York City. He probably was helped by the Underground Railroad, but because he didn't want to get anyone into trouble for assisting him, he wouldn't relate the details. "What means I adopted, what direction I traveled, and by what mode of conveyance, I must leave unexplained," he later wrote in his autobiography.

Frederick Douglass became a famous antislavery lecturer and author. He settled in Rochester, New York, where he published an antislavery newspaper called the *North Star* and turned his house into an Underground Railroad station. On occasion the Douglass home sheltered as many as eleven fugitives at once.

This painting by John Adam Houston captures the desperate fear and remarkable bravery of a solitary slave running for his freedom.

without assistance, depending solely on their own courage, intelligence, and ingenuity to find their way to freedom.

After slavery ended, a few UGRR workers, including Levi Coffin, Harriet Tubman, and William Still, wrote about their experiences. Their books and other accounts were the sources for the true stories of slave escapes in the next chapter.

William Wells Brown (1815-1884), a noted abolitionist and lecturer, was the first African American to publish a play or a novel.

Wm. W. Brown.

THREE

"I HAD CROSSED THAT LINE": TRUE UGRR STORIES

The elderly gentleman, who was a Quaker and an Underground Railroad agent, was true to his word. He hid William inside his wagon and drove him to his farm. There the man and his wife nursed William back to health. Two weeks later, when William felt well enough to move on, he told the couple that, as a slave, he had never had a last name. Since they had saved his life, they should name him.

"I shall call thee Wells Brown after myself," said the man, but William wanted to retain his first name. "Then I will call thee William Wells Brown," said the gentleman.

A few days later William Wells Brown reached Cleveland, Ohio. Feeling that he was beyond the slave hunters' grasp, he temporarily settled in Cleveland, where UGRR agents sheltered him and gave him work. For sawing firewood one family paid him a quarter, with which he bought a spelling book and a bag of candy. The family had two young boys who knew how to read and write. The boys agreed to teach William, who paid for each lesson with a few pieces of candy.

When spring arrived William found a job on a Lake Erie steamboat and began working as an Underground Railroad conductor. Over the next few years he helped transport many fugitive slaves across Lake Erie to Canada, including sixty-nine in one year. He married, and in 1836 he and his wife moved to Buffalo, New York, where they made their home into an Underground Railroad station.

The boys must have taught William well, for he became a noted author. His works included *Clotel*, the first published novel by an African American, and *The Escape*, the first published play by an African American. William Wells Brown had a great sorrow in his life, though. He spent many years trying to locate his mother, sister, and brothers but never found them.

Harriet Tubman, UGRR Conductor

Growing up in Maryland, Harriet Tubman knew all the miseries of slavery. As a young child she was hired out by her owner to a man who trapped muskrats. She spent so much time in the cold water that she became very ill. At age nine she went to work as a house slave for a Miss Susan. Besides cleaning house all day, she had to keep Miss Susan's baby quiet at night. Decades later Tubman still bore scars from whippings Miss Susan gave her whenever she fell asleep and the baby cried.

In her teens Tubman was put to work as a field slave. One night she got in the way of a fight between a young male slave and an overseer. The overseer threw an iron weight that hit her in the head, nearly killing her. Tubman's severe head injury caused her to suffer frequent seizures and powerful headaches for the rest of her life. She would fall asleep in the midst of a task or even while talking, then awaken and continue where she had left off.

In 1849, when she was about twenty-seven years old, Tubman heard a rumor that she and some siblings were about to be sold to owners in the Deep South. She convinced two of her brothers to flee with her before that happened. They had gone a short way when her brothers panicked about getting caught and punished. They turned around and convinced Tubman to return with them.

Escaped slaves who were caught were often sold to new owners in the Deep South. These were states such as Alabama, Mississippi, Georgia, and Louisiana, located in the far southern part of the country. It was very difficult for slaves to escape from the Deep South, because the Northern states and Canada were so far away. Also slaves sold to the Deep South were usually so far from relatives and friends that they had little hope of ever seeing them again.

Just days later, Tubman set out again—this time alone. As she departed she told herself, "No one will take me back alive! I shall fight for my liberty!"

Following the North Star, Tubman traveled by night. Because of her seizures and headaches, she probably had to stop from time to time to lean against a tree or lie on the ground. She was helped by the Underground Railroad on her journey. One farmer who was a UGRR agent hid Tubman in his wagon and drove her a short distance. A white woman who was apparently a Quaker also helped her, although Tubman never explained the details.

Averaging about 20 miles (32 km) a night, Tubman needed just a few days to travel about one hundred miles

(161 km) from the slave state of Maryland to the free state of Pennsylvania. On an autumn day in 1849 she walked upon free soil for the first time in her life. She later recalled that moment:

> When I found I had crossed that line, I looked at my hands to see if I was the same person. There was such a glory over everything. The Sun came like gold through the trees, and over the fields, and I felt like I was in Heaven.

Harriet Tubman settled in Philadelphia. Freedom was wonderful, yet how could she be satisfied while people dear to her remained slaves? Tubman decided to return to Maryland and lead friends and relatives away. She investigated and learned the locations of the Underground Railroad stations between Maryland and Pennsylvania. Between 1850 and

Harriet Tubman (c.1820-1913) became known as the Moses of her people, because she led so many to freedom.

1860 Tubman made at least thirteen trips as an Underground Railroad conductor. She led at least seventy family members and friends to freedom, and gave instructions to many more who found their way north on their own.

Just 5 feet (1.5 meters) tall, disabled by the head injury, and unable to read and write, Tubman seemed like an unlikely heroine. How could she free so many slaves without getting caught?

To prevent herself from being recognized, she sometimes masked her identity by walking hunched over, as if she were very old. Who would suspect that the elderly woman, bent with age, was Underground Railroad conductor Harriet Tubman? Once she pretended she could read to throw off suspicion when she ran into her old master on a train. She often walked separately from the people she was leading northward. That way, if she suddenly fell asleep, she wouldn't put the whole group in danger. She was also very resourceful. Several times when slave hunters were on her trail she temporarily led her passengers *south*. That relieved suspicions about her, for everyone knew that escaped slaves headed *north*.

Using the language of the Underground Railroad, Harriet Tubman once said about herself: "I never ran my train off the track, and I never lost a passenger."

Thomas Garrett, Stationmaster

Over a forty-year period, Quaker merchant Thomas Garrett aided 2,500 escaped slaves at his home and office in Wilmington, Delaware. Besides feeding and sheltering fugitives, he sometimes guided them the last several miles northward into Pennsylvania, so he was both an Underground Railroad stationmaster and conductor. He often assisted Harriet Tubman, who regularly stopped at his home or office. In 1856 Garrett helped Tubman and a group of fugitive slaves survive a dangerous predicament.

The Market Street Bridge crossing the Christina River in Wilmington was closely guarded by police and slave hunters looking for fugitives. In the fall of 1856 Garrett received word that Harriet Tubman was on the south side of the bridge with five escaped slaves. Their owners had offered large rewards for these slaves, so the bridge was crawling with police and slave hunters. Could Thomas figure out a way that Tubman and her five passengers could cross the bridge?

Garrett hired some bricklayers and in the morning he had them cross the bridge from north to south in two wagons as though they were going to work. That evening after sunset, the bricklayers crossed the bridge from south to north, as if they were heading home after their day's work. Neither the police nor the slave hunters suspected that anything was amiss, and they let the wagons pass without checking them. What they didn't know was that the wagon had a false bottom, and

Harriet Tubman (*far left*) poses with a group of former slaves. She helped them to escape to freedom on the Underground Railroad.

hiding beneath the bricks were the most famous Underground Railroad conductor and five slaves in her care. After getting through this crisis with Thomas Garrett's help, Harriet Tubman took the fugitives all the way to Canada.

Henry Brown, Cargo

Henry Brown and his wife, Nancy, hired their own time in Richmond, Virginia—he worked in a tobacco factory, and she took in laundry. Married for twelve years, Henry and Nancy were allowed to live together as a family with their three children.

Then, one summer day in 1848, Henry came home from the tobacco factory for lunch and discovered that his wife and children were gone. Needing money, their owner had sold Nancy and the children to a North Carolina planter.

Brown was determined to escape, then locate and free his family. During the next few months he formed a plan with an Underground Railroad ticket agent named Samuel A. Smith. They obtained a large box, drilled three small holes in it, and packed a water container and biscuits inside. Smith, who was a shoe dealer, addressed the box as if it were a load of shoes he was sending to Philadelphia. Meanwhile he telegraphed Underground Railroad agent William Still in Philadelphia and informed him that a "case of goods" was on its way. After Brown climbed into the box, Smith nailed it shut and had it taken to the train depot.

For the next twenty-nine hours the box containing Henry Brown rode in trains and steamboats 275 miles (442.5 km) between Richmond and Philadelphia. Brown was cramped in his box. The three small holes provided little air. Sometimes he rode upside down. But early on a spring morning in 1849 a carriage driver picked up the box at the Philadelphia train station and brought it to William Still, who was waiting at the Pennsylvania Anti-Slavery Society office with three other

UGRR agents. When Still and his friends removed the lid, out popped Henry Brown, who fainted from excitement. He awoke to find that he was a free man in Philadelphia. Because of the odd way that he arrived, William Still gave Henry the nickname "Box" Brown.

William Still took Brown to his home to recover from the ordeal of being locked in a wooden box for twenty-nine hours. Still then sent him farther north to Boston, a safer city for fugitive slaves. Brown lectured in Massachusetts and Maine

Henry Brown emerges after many grueling hours as human cargo. He later wrote an autobiography, *Narrative of the Life of Henry Box Brown.*

about his experiences, raising money to buy his family out of bondage. However, it appears that he was never able to free his family, and in the mid-1850s, Henry "Box" Brown disappeared from history.

As for Samuel A. Smith, after his success with Henry Brown, he boxed up more slaves and shipped them to the North. But two slaves sent by Smith were discovered in their crates, and the Underground Railroad ticket agent was arrested and sent to the penitentiary in Richmond, Virginia. During his seven years in prison, Smith survived a severe stabbing, probably by a proslavery inmate. Following his release Smith went to Philadelphia, where he made a speech saying that he felt proud to have helped Brown and a few others escape slavery.

Harriet Tubman leads a group of slaves across the border into Canada to a new life of freedom. Slavery was outlawed in Canada in 1834.

THE FUGITIVE SLAVE LAW OF 1850 AND THE UGRR

The United States was only a few years old when Congress made a law allowing owners to capture slaves who fled to the North. As discussed earlier, the Fugitive Slave Act of 1793 permitted owners and slave hunters to capture escaped slaves and return them to the South. But because of the trouble and expense of catching fugitives, not many slaves were recovered as a result of this law.

Since slaves were worth an average of about $500, each one who ran away cost his or her owner a small fortune. Between 1801 and 1850 perhaps 100,000 slaves worth a total of about $50 million escaped from the South. Southern slave owners wanted the federal government to pass a law making it easier for them to recover fugitive slaves.

THE SHRINK-ING VALUE OF RUNAWAYS

A slave who had run away was likely to do so again. Consequently the slave lost value. Instead of $500, he or she might be worth only $200. A slave who had run away repeatedly couldn't be sold for much at all, because who wanted to buy goods that might suddenly vanish?

By the mid-1800s people in the North and the South were arguing bitterly over issues relating to slavery. California was ready for statehood. Would it be a slave state, as Southerners wanted, or a free state, as Northerners demanded? Another dispute was over the fact that it was legal for slaves to be bought and sold in Washington, D.C. Antislavery people called it shameful that our country's capital allowed slave auctions. Proslavery people argued that Washington, D.C., was in the South and should continue to allow slave sales like other Southern cities.

The biggest source of friction involved the Underground Railroad. White Southerners demanded that the U.S. government do more to stop the Underground Railroad from aiding escaped slaves. Northern abolitionists argued that it was wrong to own another human being; therefore, by helping fugitive slaves, the UGRR was doing the right thing.

In 1850 the North and the South made a compromise, which meant that each region got its way on some issues and lost out on others. As part of the Compromise of 1850, California entered the Union as a free state. Buying and selling slaves was ended in Washington, D.C. An important new law was also passed to weaken the Underground Railroad and help owners capture runaway slaves.

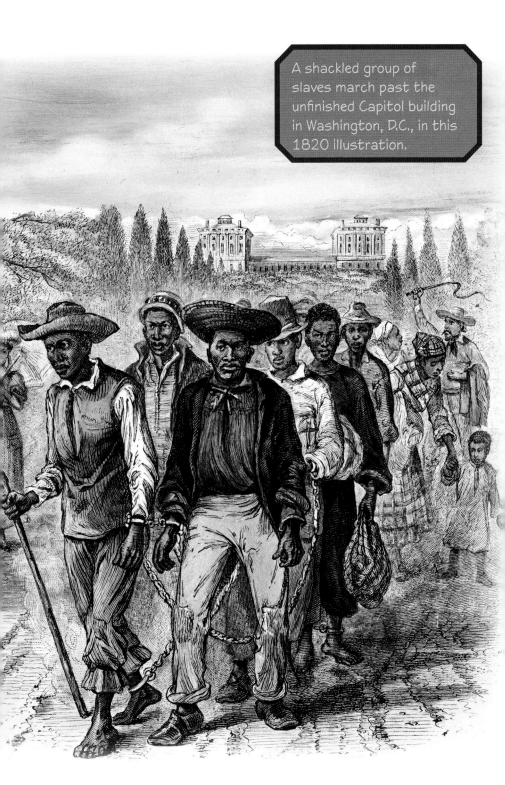

A shackled group of slaves march past the unfinished Capitol building in Washington, D.C., in this 1820 illustration.

People who wanted to end slavery immediately were called *abolitionists*. The word comes from *abolish*, which means to get rid of or destroy. Although most white abolitionists lived in the North, there were some in the South, too, such as the shoe merchant Samuel A. Smith. Southern slaveholders routinely referred to abolitionists as "the damned abolitionists."

The Fugitive Slave Law of 1850 made it a federal offense to "harbor or conceal" an escaped slave. Furthermore anyone who aided a fugitive slave could be fined $2,000 and jailed for six months. In addition law officers were ordered to help owners track down and arrest fugitive slaves. Another clause said that, if asked, "all citizens" and "bystanders" were "commanded to aid and assist" authorities in seizing runaway slaves. In other words everyone—whether for or against slavery—could be called on to help capture fugitive slaves.

The "Higher Law"

The Fugitive Slave Law of 1850 pleased white Southerners, because the U.S. government finally seemed to be helping them retrieve escaped slaves. Opponents of slavery were furious, since the new law overturned all the state laws forbidding slavery in the North. Now fugitive slaves weren't safe anywhere on American soil. Abolitionists especially hated the "bystander" clause, which made all Americans potential slave hunters.

Abolitionist ministers and lecturers accused the U.S. government of passing an evil law just to please slaveholders. They advised people to ignore the new Fugitive Slave Law,

Slave hunters earned their living by tracking down and capturing runaways and then collecting rewards from slaveholders for their return.

and spoke of a "higher law"that Americans should obey. Some would call this the "law of right and wrong," "God's law," or the Golden Rule. According to the higher law everyone deserved to be free, and all people should work to make that happen.

Back during the time of the American Revolution, Boston had been America's most rebellious town. The Boston Tea Party and the Boston Massacre took place there, and the war's first battle was fought in nearby Lexington, Massachusetts. Seventy-five years after the war for independence, the great-grandchildren of the Revolutionary patriots made Boston America's leading abolitionist town. Soon after President Millard Fillmore signed the Fugitive Slave Law into effect on September 18, 1850, Bostonians showed what they thought of it.

Send in the Marines

The year the law was enacted a slave named Shadrach Minkins fled Virginia. He settled in Boston. In early 1851 U.S. marshals arrested Minkins for being a runaway slave. Instead of helping the marshals as the Fugitive Slave Law ordered, Bostonians took Minkins from them by force. They sent him via the Underground Railroad to Canada, which had outlawed slavery in 1834. Shadrach Minkins married and raised a family in Canada, where he lived for the rest of his life.

President Fillmore didn't want Bostonians to get away with defying the new law. He insisted that the ringleaders who freed Minkins be prosecuted. A number of them were arrested. However, antislavery juries in Boston acquitted them of wrongdoing.

Thomas Sims was a seventeen-year-old slave from Georgia who escaped to Boston in 1851. That spring Sims was arrested under the Fugitive Slave Law and ordered by a court to be returned to his owner. Because Bostonians threatened to grab Sims from the authorities as had happened with Minkins, the U.S. government sent in the Marines. The troops escorted Sims through the streets to a warship that returned him to Georgia.

Boston's most violent episode concerning the Fugitive Slave Law involved Anthony Burns, who escaped from Virginia in early 1853. That spring Burns was arrested as a fugitive slave, but Bostonians rioted in the streets and attacked authorities who intended to return him to bondage. In the fighting a deputy U.S. marshal was stabbed to death. Two thousand U.S. troops were needed to escort Burns to the ship that returned him to his master.

Boston abolitionists did not give up on freeing Anthony Burns. They raised $1,300 and bought his freedom from his master. In 1855 Burns returned to Boston as a free man.

Syracuse, New York, was the site of a famous rescue from the clutches of the Fugitive Slave Law. William Henry,

KIDNAPPED INTO SLAVERY Slave owners often complained about valuable slaves running away. What they didn't mention was that many rich planters increased their slave holdings by buying black people who had been kidnapped into slavery. Often what happened was that a free black person would be kidnapped, taken to the South, and sold at an auction. If the person complained that he was a free black, he would probably get a whipping just as a reminder that he was now a slave. How many thousands of free blacks were kidnapped into slavery is unknown.

nicknamed "Jerry," was an escaped slave from Missouri who worked as a barrel maker in Syracuse. In the fall of 1851 Henry was arrested by police and federal marshals, but a crowd of abolitionists broke into the building where Henry was being held and liberated him. With the Underground Railroad's help, Henry secretly fled to Canada. Although twenty-six of Henry's rescuers were accused of breaking the Fugitive Slave Law, only one was convicted and sent to jail.

Making Life Miserable for Slave Hunters

Abolitionists countered the Fugitive Slave Law with their own legal moves. Wherever slave hunters pursued runaways, abolitionists accused them of breaking every law in the book. For example, when strangers came onto his property looking for escaped slaves, Levi Coffin had them arrested for trespassing. If slave hunters "attempted to enter my house" looking for runaway slaves, explained Coffin, "I would have them arrested as kidnappers."

The case of Ellen and William Craft was an example of abolitionists using laws to strike back at slave hunters. The Crafts were a married couple in Macon, Georgia, who carried out a daring escape. Ellen, a light-skinned African American, dressed in male clothing and pretended to be a white man heading North with his slave, William. The masquerade worked, and the Crafts traveled by train and steamboat to freedom in Philadelphia. With the help of the Underground Railroad, they later settled in Boston. Just a month after the Fugitive Slave Law took effect, Georgia slave hunters John Knight and Willis Hughes came to Boston to capture the Crafts.

Boston's abolitionists made life miserable for Knight and Hughes. Five days after arriving in Boston, the two men were arrested for calling William Craft a slave. By Massachusetts law William was a free man, and so the slave hunters had to post bail or be jailed for slander. Two days later Knight and

Hughes were arrested for planning to take the Crafts back to Georgia, which Bostonians considered kidnapping. Once again the two Georgians had to post bail to keep from being locked behind bars.

Instead of bringing Ellen and William Craft back to Macon, Knight and Hughes had to sneak out of Boston to avoid being jailed themselves. Back in Georgia, Hughes complained to a newspaper that Bostonians had dogged his every step. He had been arrested for "smoking in the streets, swearing in the streets, carrying concealed weapons, driving fast through the streets, and for passing Cambridge Bridge without paying the toll." One would have thought that

HOW NORTHERNERS HELPED SLAVERY CONTINUE

Northerners helped keep slavery alive by buying goods produced by slaves. They wore clothing made of cotton grown by slaves. They used tobacco, ate rice and sugar, and dyed materials with indigo produced by slaves. For several years before the Civil War, Levi Coffin headed a Quaker organization that avoided using anything produced by slaves. Coffin explained: "The object of the slaveholder was to make money by selling the cotton, sugar, etc., produced by his slaves, and without a market for these he would have been deprived of the great motive for holding the negroes in bondage." However, not enough people refused to use goods produced by slaves to do much damage to the slavery system.

In case she was asked to sign papers during her escape to the North, Ellen Craft (1826-1891) wrapped her right arm in a sling to hide that she was unable to write.

the two Georgia slave hunters, and not the Crafts, were the lawbreakers. That was exactly how Bostonians viewed the situation.

Meanwhile the Fugitive Slave Law did not wreck or even slow down the Underground Railroad. In fact it did the opposite. Despite the risks, most Underground Railroad agents were so angered by the new law that they redoubled their efforts to help runaway slaves. The Underground Railroad was busier than ever during the 1850s, but with one difference. Instead of conducting runaways to the Northern states, the UGRR led many of them all the way to Canada, where slave catchers weren't permitted to track them down.

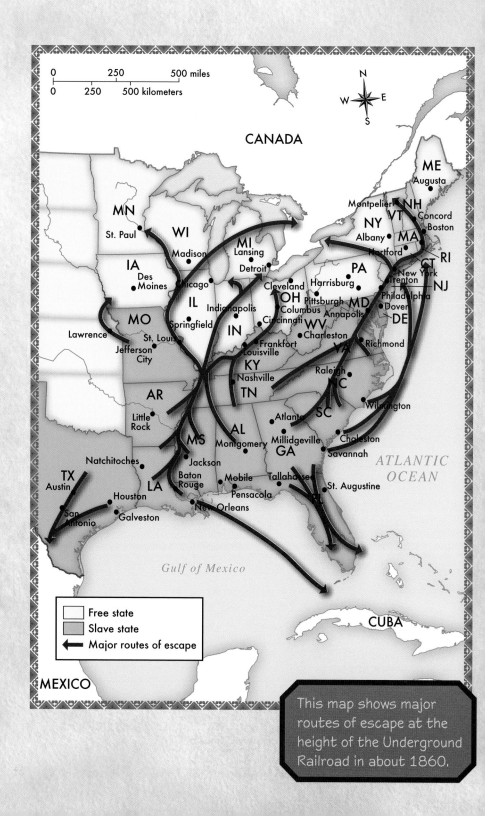

This map shows major routes of escape at the height of the Underground Railroad in about 1860.

THE END OF SLAVERY

To Southern slaveholders the Fugitive Slave Law of 1850 was a bitter disappointment. They had hoped that all Americans—even abolitionists—would obey the act because it was the law of the land. That didn't happen. They had also hoped that the law would reduce the number of slaves who escaped and increase the number of runaways who were captured. That didn't happen either. Thanks largely to the Underground Railroad, during the 1850s more slaves escaped than ever before—probably more than 30,000 over the course of the decade.

Slaveholders had two targets to blame for the Fugitive Slave Law's ineffectiveness. First they blamed the Northern abolitionists. Antislavery Americans seemed to think they could choose which laws they would obey and which they wouldn't. For example, although the Fugitive Slave Law made the Underground Railroad illegal, abolitionists claimed that UGRR workers were heroes for helping slaves escape.

HOW MANY SLAVES RAN AWAY?

No one knows even roughly how many slaves ran away. For one thing owners didn't always admit that some of their slaves escaped. There were also several ways to count slaves who had run away. Some counts included slaves who were caught and brought back, while others counted only successful escape attempts. How do you figure in people like Harriet Tubman's brothers, who escaped but got scared and turned back? Because of the different ways to count and the lack of accurate records, historians say that anywhere from 60,000 to 180,000 slaves escaped between 1800 and 1860.

Slave owners also blamed the U.S. government. The government made a few halfhearted attempts to enforce the Fugitive Slave Law. However, Northern judges and juries often ignored the evidence and let accused violators off with light penalties or no punishments at all. Southerners felt that the U.S. government had made a law it never intended to enforce.

Abolitionists were just as disappointed with the Fugitive Slave Law as the slaveholders were. Mexico had ended slavery in the 1820s. Canada and other parts of the British Empire had abolished slavery in 1834. France had freed the slaves of its New World colonies in 1848. How could the country that called itself "the land of the free" allow slavery to continue?

The Civil War Decides the Slavery Issue

As the 1860s began, the slavery issue was tearing the nation apart. Abraham Lincoln, who became president in 1861, had predicted that this would happen. In a speech he made in 1858 Lincoln had said, "I believe this government cannot endure, permanently half slave and half free."

The war that Americans had feared but expected finally began in 1861. Called the Civil War, it pitted the Southern or Confederate states against the Northern or Union states. The war was fought largely over slavery. Another major issue was "states' rights." The South claimed that states had the right to decide about various issues, including slavery, without interference from the U.S. government.

The Underground Railroad helped the North win the war. Of the 2.1 million soldiers and sailors on the Northern side, 215,000, or about a tenth, were black men. Most of the African-American troops were either runaway slaves from the South who had escaped on the Underground Railroad or descendants of runaway slaves. Because they were fighting for the freedom of their people, the black troops were among the toughest of the Union forces. They served in all-black regiments, fought in more than two hundred battles and skirmishes, and included more than twenty men who won the Medal of Honor for heroism in the Civil War.

For example, Sergeant William Carney, an escaped slave from Virginia, won the Medal of Honor for his bravery in a battle at Fort Wagner in South Carolina. Carney led a charge and survived the battle despite suffering four wounds. Famed Underground Railroad conductor Harriet Tubman served as a Union scout and spy and was one of just a few women who fought in the war. The most important skirmish in which she took part was the Combahee River Raid in South Carolina. Tubman did advance scouting along the river. Then, on the night of June 2, 1863, she and Colonel James Montgomery led 150 African-American troops up the river in three gunboats. The vessels dropped off small groups of soldiers who burned Confederate property and freed nearly one thousand slaves.

The Combahee River Raid was the first battle in U.S. history that was planned and commanded by a woman.

Thousands of other African-American and white soldiers did their part in the Union victory. After four years of fighting, peace between the North and the South was made in April of 1865. Eight months later, in December of 1865, the Thirteenth Amendment to the U.S. Constitution was ratified, ending

African-American troops served with distinction during the Civil War. This November 1865 photo shows the 107th Colored Infantry at Fort Corcoran, Arlington, Virginia.

slavery within the United States. Good people like Samuel A. Smith, William Still, Harriet Tubman, Levi and Katie Coffin, Thomas Garrett, and Frederick Douglass had finally achieved their goal, and so the Underground Railroad was no longer needed. At the end of his book Levi Coffin described a celebration in Cincinnati, at which

This gallery of a dozen antislavery activists includes Frederick Douglass, Thomas Garrett, and William Still.

I said that I had held the position of President of the Underground Railroad for more than thirty years. Amid much applause, I resigned my office and declared the operations of the Underground Railroad at an end.

Those Who Remained Slaves

Only a small fraction of slaves escaped. For example, in 1850 there were 3.2 million slaves. If three thousand slaves escaped that year, it means that only about one in a thousand slaves got away from their owners. We should remember that those who never had the chance to escape slavery were heroes, too. They raised families, forged strong friendships, and found ways to enjoy life—despite the fact that they lived as slaves from birth to death.

TIME LINE

1492–1493—On his famous voyage to the New World, Christopher Columbus begins enslaving the Indians.

1500s—While settling the Americas, Europeans enslave and wipe out huge numbers of Indians.

1619—Twenty black slaves arrive in Jamestown, Virginia, marking the start of African-American slavery in what later became the United States.

1663—First slave revolt in what became the United States takes place in Gloucester County, Virginia.

1700—Out of total population of 250,000 in England's American colonies, 30,000 are black slaves.

1712—New York City's slave rebellion; nine whites are killed and twenty-one slaves are executed.

1750—Out of 1.2 million people in thirteen colonies, nearly a quarter million are black slaves.

1776—The United States declares its independence from England.

1780—Massachusetts becomes the first state to outlaw slavery.

1784—Quakers become first religious denomination in the United States to end slaveholding among its members.

1800— Slave rebellion led by Gabriel Prosser ends with the hanging of Prosser and dozens of other slaves.

1822— Slave revolt led by Denmark Vesey ends with the hanging of Vesey and dozens of followers.

1831—Nat Turner leads the bloodiest slave revolt in U.S. history in Southampton County, Virginia; fifty-five whites and more than fifty blacks die; out of revenge, white gangs kill hundreds of African Americans.

1830s and 1840s—Rise of the Underground Railroad.

1834—William Wells Brown escapes slavery; he becomes an Underground Railroad conductor.

1849—Famous Underground Railroad escape of Henry "Box" Brown.

1850—Fugitive Slave Law helps owners retrieve runaway slaves but greatly angers abolitionists, who defy it.

1851—Bostonians are so enraged over the Fugitive Slave Law that in order to return runaway slave Thomas Sims to Georgia the U.S. government sends in the Marines.

1853—Bostonians attack authorities who try to return fugitive slave Anthony Burns to Virginia; a deputy U.S. marshal is stabbed to death.

1857—Famed Underground Railroad conductor Harriet Tubman leads her parents out of slavery.

1860—Harriet Tubman makes her last trip as an Underground Railroad conductor; since 1800 as many as 180,000 slaves have escaped.

1861–1865—North and South fight the Civil War, largely over slavery.

1865—In December, the Thirteenth Amendment is approved, ending slavery in the United States.

1872—William Still publishes *The Underground Railroad*, which provides much information about its secret workings.

1876—Levi Coffin publishes *Reminiscences of Levi Coffin*, which also provides a picture of the UGRR.

1913—Harriet Tubman dies at age ninety-one.

1965—One hundredth anniversary of the end of the Civil War and the freeing of the slaves.

2015—One hundred and fiftieth anniversary of the end of the Civil War and the freeing of the slaves.

NOTES

All websites were accessed between May and June, 2010.

Introduction

P .5, par. 1, "Try to get your liberty!": William Wells Brown, *Sketches of Places and People Abroad* (Cleveland: Jewett, 1855), p. 21.

p. 6, par. 1, "seize or arrest": "Fugitive Slave Act of 1793," www.ushistory.org/presidentshouse/history/slaveact1793.htm.

p. 6, par. 3, "Soon, an elderly man . . .": William Wells Brown, *Narrative of William W. Brown, a Fugitive Slave* (Boston: Anti-Slavery Office), 1847, p. 101.

p. 7, par. 3, "After William had been waiting . . .": *Narrative of William W. Brown*, 1847, p. 102.

Chapter I

p. 9, par. 1, "Now [that] I've been free . . .": Benjamin Drew, *A North-Side View of Slavery; The Refugee: or the Narratives of Fugitive Slaves in Canada* (New York: Johnson Reprint Corporation, 1968 [reprint of 1856 edition]), p. 30.

p. 9, par. 2, "offer to share with anyone" and "they would make fine servants. . . .": Howard Zinn, "Columbus, the Indians, and Human Progress," www.thirdworldtraveler.com/Zinn/Columbus_PeoplesHx.html

p. 10, par. 2, "About 2 million of them died . . .": "The African Slave Trade and the Middle Passage," www.pbs.org/wgbh/aia/part1/1narr4.html

p. 12, sidebar, "were either excluded from railway cars . . .": Eugene Berwanger, quoted in "Go Home, Johnny Reb," seminal.firedoglake.com/diary/50566

p. 13, par. 4, "The crowd collected round . . .": Josiah Henson, *Father Henson's Story of His Own Life* (Williamstown, MA: Corner House Publishers, 1973 [reprint of 1858 edition]), pp. 11–13.

p. 18, par. 1, "I have often been awakened . . .": Frederick Douglass, *Narrative of the Life of Frederick Douglass, an American Slave, Written by Himself* (Cambridge, MA: The Belknap Press of Harvard University Press, 1988 [reprint of 1845 edition]), p. 28.

Chapter II

p. 21, par. 2 "The earliest known slave revolt . . .": "Slave Rebellion," www.footnote.com/page/1437_slave_rebellion/

p. 21, par. 3, "For example, during New York City's . . .": "Slave Rebellion," www.footnote.com/page/1437_slave_rebellion/

p. 22, par. 1, "Gabriel Prosser, a slave . . .": "Nat Turner: a Troublesome Property: Slave Rebellions: A Timeline," www. pbs.org/independentlens/natturner/slave_rebellions.html

p. 23, par. 1, "Twenty-two years later, Denmark Vesey . . .": "Nat Turner: a Troublesome Property: Slave Rebellions: a Timeline," www.pbs.org/independentlens/natturner/slave_ rebellions.html

p. 24, par. 1, "Nat Turner led the bloodiest . . .": "Nat Turner: a Troublesome Property," www.pbs.org/independentlens/ natturner/

p. 25, sidebar, "the Fugitive Slave Act of 1793 allowed . . .": "Feb. 12, 1793: Congress Enacts First Fugitive Slave Law," www. history.com/this-day-in-history/2/12?catld=6

p. 27, par. 2, "The North Star—blessed be God . . .": Henson, *Father Henson's Story of His Own Life,* pp. 102–103.

p. 27, sidebar, "Ona Judge, Runaway . . .": Evelyn Gerson, "Ona Judge Staines: Escape from Washington," www.seacoastnh. com/blackhistory/ona.html

p. 28, par. 3, "How did the Underground Railroad get its start?" "Underground Railroad," www.spartacus.schoolnet.co.uk/ USASunderground.htm

p. 28, par. 4, "There must be an underground railroad . . .": "The Levi Coffin House" (pamphlet, unnumbered pages).

p. 30, par. 1, "on the UGRR . . .": Levi Coffin, *Reminiscences of Levi Coffin* (Richmond, IN: Friends United Press, 1991 [reprint of 1876 edition]), p. 69.

p. 30, par. 2, "the train was run off the track . . .": "History Alive! The Underground Railroad in Wisconsin," www.teachingwithstories.com/teachers/quotes.htm

p. 31, sidebar, "In 1784 the Quakers became the first . . ." *Reminiscences of Levi Coffin*, from Foreword by Ben Richmond, pp. xvi–xvii.

p. 31, par. 2, "A lantern attached to a hitching post . . .": "The Underground Railroad," www.nationalgeographic.com/railroad/j4.html

p. 32, sidebar, par. 1, "a kind and tender-hearted . . .": Douglass, *Narrative of the Life of Frederick Douglass,* p. 63.

p. 32, sidebar, par. 1, "What means I adopted . . .": *Narrative of the Life of Frederick Douglass*, p. 143.

Chapter III

p. 35, par. 2, "I shall call thee Wells Brown . . .": Brown, *Narrative of William W. Brown, a Fugitive Slave,* p. 105.

p. 35, par. 3, "he bought a spelling book and a bag of candy.": Stephen Lucasi, "William Wells Brown's Narrative," www.accessmylibrary.com/cons2/summary_0286-34632206_ITM

p. 36, par. 1, "including sixty-nine in one year.": *Narrative of William W. Brown, 1847*, p. 109.

p. 36, par. 4, "Tubman's severe head injury . . .": Sarah Bradford, *Tubman: The Moses of Her People* (New York: Lockwood, 1886), p. 15.

p. 37, par. 2, "No one will take me back alive!" Bradford: *Tubman: The Moses of Her People*, p. 29.

p. 38, par. 1, "When I found I had crossed that line . . .": "Harriet Tubman—A Story That Must Be Told," www.easternshore.com/esguide/tubman.html

p. 39, par. 1, "Tubman made at least thirteen . . .": Kate Clifford Larson, "Bound for the Promised Land: Harriet Tubman," www.Tubmantubmanbiography.com/id6.html

p. 39, par. 5, "Over a forty-year-period . . .": Judith Bentley, *"Dear Friend": Thomas Garrett and William Still, Collaborators on the Underground Railroad* (New York: Cobblehill, 1997), p. 89.

p. 40, par.1, "The Market Street Bridge . . .": Bentley, *"Dear Friend"*, pp. 43–44.

p. 41, par. 2, "Then, one summer day . . .": Henry Brown, *Narrative of the Life of Henry Box Brown,* (Manchester, England: Lee and Glynn, 1851), p. 40.

p. 41, par. 3, "They obtained a large box . . .": *Narrative of the Life of Henry Box Brown*, p. 53.

p. 42, par. 1, "out popped Henry Brown . . ." *Narrative of the Life of Henry Box Brown*, p. 57.

p. 43, par. 1. "As for Samuel A. Smith . . ." "Henry Box Brown," encylopedia.jrank.org/articles/pages/4138/Brown-Henry-Box-1815.html

Chapter IV

p. 45, par. 2, "Between 1801 and 1850, perhaps 100,000 slaves . . .": David Taft Terry, "Fugitive Slaves in Maryland," www.mdoe.org/fugitiveslaves.html .

p. 48, par. 1, "The Fugitive Slave Law of 1850 . . .": "Fugitive Slave Act 1850," www.nationalcenter.org/FugitiveSlaveAct.html

p. 50, par. 1, "spoke of a 'higher law' . . .": Jennifer Hahn, "Higher Law and Moral Relativism," www.victorianweb.org/courses/nonfiction/thoreau/hahn.html

p. 50, par. 3, "a slave named Shadrach Minkins . . .": "Shadrach Minkins Seized," massmoments.org/index.cfm?mid=53

p. 50, par. 5, "Thomas Sims was . . .": "When Boston Awoke," www.boston.com/bostonglobe/ideas/articles/2010/04/11/when_boston_awoke/

p. 51, par. 1, "Boston's most violent episode . . .": "Fugitive Slave Anthony Burns Arrested," massmoments.org/moment.cfm?mid=153

p. 51, par. 3, "William Henry, nicknamed . . .": Paul Rosenberg, "The Heroes of the Underground Railroad" (in section on Charles Augustus Wheaton), www.fr33agents.com/1184/the-heroes-of-the-underground-railroad/

p. 52, par. 2, "If slave hunters 'attempted to enter . . .'": Levi Coffin, *Reminiscences of Levi Coffin* (Richmond, IN: Friends United Press, 1991 [reprint of 1876 edition]), p. 78.

p. 52, par. 3, "The case of Ellen and William Craft . . . how Bostonians viewed the situation.": Judith Bloom Fradin and Dennis Brindell Fradin, *5,000 Miles to Freedom: Ellen and William Craft's Flight from Slavery* (Washington, D.C.: National Geographic, 2006), pp. 53–57.

p. 53, sidebar, "The object of the slave holder . . .": Coffin, *Reminiscences of Levi Coffin*, p. 188.

Chapter V

p. 57, par. 1, "during the 1850s more slaves escaped . . .": "The Fugitive Slave Act and the Underground Railroad," www.math.buffalo.edu/~sww/0history/UndergroundRailRoad.html

p. 58, sidebar, "Because of the different ways to count . . .": "Myths of the Underground Railroad," teacher.scholastic.com/activities/bhistory/underground_railroad/myths.htm; "The Underground Railroad," www.osblackhistory.com/underground.php

p. 51, par. 1, "In a speech he made in 1858 . . .": "House Divided Speech," showcase.netins.net/web/creative/lincoln/speeches/house.htm

p. 59, par. 3, "Of the 2.1 million . . .": "Black Soldiers in the Civil War," www.archives.gov/education/lessons/blacks-civil-war/

p. 59, par. 3, "included more than twenty men . . .": "African American Medal of Honor Recipients—Civil War," www.itd.nps.gov/cwss/history/aa_medals.htm

p. 59, par. 4, "For example, Sergeant William Carney . . .":
"Sergeant Carney's Flag," www.homeofheroes.com/
hallofheroes/1st_floor/flag1bfa_hist5carney.html

p. 59, par. 4, "The most important skirmish . . .": Earl Conrad,
"General Tubman," www.Tubmantubman.com/tubman2.html

p. 63, par. 1, "I said that I had held . . .": Coffin, *Reminiscences of
Levi Coffin*, pp. 389–390.

GLOSSARY

abolitionists—People who wanted to end slavery immediately.

antislavery—Against slavery.

auctions—Events for buying and selling goods at which the people who bid the most money get to purchase the items.

authorities—People in charge.

autobiography—A book about a person's life written by that person.

bondage—Another word for slavery.

colonies—Settlements made by people outside the boundaries of their original home country.

compromise—An agreement by which each side gets what it wants on some issues and loses out on other issues.

conductors (Underground Railroad)—People like Harriet Tubman who led escaped slaves northward.

denomination (religious)—A particular religion.

depot—A building for train passengers and/or freight.

fugitive (slave)—A slave who has run away.

indigo—A plant from which a blue dye, also called indigo, is made.

oppressed—Mistreated and deprived of human rights.

overseer—A field boss who oversaw or supervised the slaves' work.

prejudice—Dislike of a group of people because of such things as their race, religion, or sex.

proslavery—In favor of slavery.

segregated—Refers to the separation of groups of people, especially by race.

slander—A false statement that is damaging to a person's reputation.

slave—A person who is owned by another person.

slave hunters—People who tracked down slaves for pay.

UGRR—Abbreviation for *Underground Railroad*.

Underground Railroad—The informal network of houses and other hiding places where escaped slaves could eat and rest on their northward journey; the term was also applied to the people involved in helping escaped slaves.

FURTHER
INFORMATION

BOOKS

Calkhoven, Laurie. *Harriet Tubman: Leading the Way to Freedom*. New York: Sterling, 2008.

Hinton, KaaVonia. *The Story of the Underground Railroad*. Hockessin, DE: Mitchell Lane Publishers, 2010.

Huey, Lois Miner. *American Archaeology Uncovers the Underground Railroad*. New York: Marshall Cavendish Benchmark, 2010.

Lassieur, Allison. *The Underground Railroad: An Interactive History Adventure*. Mankato, MN: Capstone Press, 2008.

Malaspina, Ann. *The Underground Railroad: The Journey to Freedom*. New York: Chelsea House, 2010.

Sterngass, Jon. *Frederick Douglass*. New York: Chelsea House, 2009.

WEBSITES

A PBS site with plenty of information on slavery and the Underground Railroad:

www.pbs.org/wgbh/aia/part4/4p2944.html

The National Park Service's "Aboard the Underground Railroad" site offers background on the Underground Railroad and on historic places and people connected with it:

www.cr.nps.gov/nr/travel/underground/

This interactive National Geographic site about the Underground Railroad re-creates what it was like to be a runaway slave:

www.nationalgeographic.com/railroad/

BIBLIOGRAPHY

Bentley, Judith. *"Dear Friend": Thomas Garrett and William Still, Collaborators on the Underground Railroad.* New York: Cobblehill, 1997.

Bradford, Sarah. *Harriet Tubman: The Moses of Her People* (1886 edition of 1869 book *Scenes in the Life of Harriet Tubman*). Secaucus, N.J.: The Citadel Press, 1974.

Brown, Henry. *Narrative of Henry Box Brown.* Philadelphia: Rhistoric Publications, 1969 (reprint of 1849 edition).

Coffin, Levi. *Reminiscences of Levi Coffin* (reprint of 1876 edition). Richmond, IN: Friends United Press, 1991.

Conrad, Earl. *Harriet Tubman.* Washington, D.C.: The Associated Publishers, 1943.

Craft, William, and Ellen Craft. *Running a Thousand Miles for Freedom.* New York: Arno Press and the *New York Times*, 1969 (reprint of 1860 edition).

Douglass, Frederick. *Narrative of the Life of Frederick Douglass, an American Slave, Written by Himself* (reprint of 1845 edition). Cambridge, MA: The Belknap Press of Harvard University Press, 1988.

Farrison, William. *William Wells Brown: Author and Reformer.* Chicago: University of Chicago Press, 1969.

Henson, Josiah. *Father Henson's Story of His Own Life* (reprint of 1858 edition). Williamstown, MA: Corner House Publishers, 1973.

Jefferson, Paul, ed. *The Travels of William Wells Brown* (includes reprint of 1847 edition of *Narrative of William W. Brown, A Fugitive Slave*). Edinburgh, Scotland: Edinburgh University Press, 1991.

Still, William. *The Underground Railroad* (reprint of 1872 edition). New York: Arno Press and the *New York Times*, 1968.

Two Biographies by African-American Women (includes reprint of 1856 edition of *Biography of an American Bondman* by Josephine Brown). New York: Oxford University Press, 1991.

INDEX

ABOUT THE AUTHOR

Dennis Fradin is the author of 150 books, some of them written with his wife, Judith Bloom Fradin. Their book for Clarion, *The Power of One: Daisy Bates and the Little Rock Nine*, was named a Golden Kite Honor Book. Another of Dennis's well-known books is *Let It Begin Here! Lexington & Concord: First Battles of the American Revolution*, published by Walker. Other books by the Fradins include *Jane Addams: Champion of Democracy* for Clarion and *5,000 Miles to Freedom: Ellen and William Craft's Flight from Slavery* for National Geographic Children's Books. Their latest project for National Geographic is the *Witness to Disaster* series about natural disasters. Dennis's first series for Marshall Cavendish Benchmark was *Turning Points in U.S. History*. A title from that series, *Hurricane Katrina*, was noted as an Honor Book by the Society of School Librarians International. The Fradins also wrote *Money Smart*, a series on financial literacy for kids published by Marshall Cavendish Benchmark. They have three grown children and seven grandchildren.